JUMP INTO SPORTS

Basketball

by Bob Temple

Basketball is a fun game to play. It takes lots of different skills.

Basketball players use strength, speed, and teamwork.

The game is played on a basketball **court**. There is a hoop at each end of the court. Each team tries to make **baskets** into one hoop.

Most basketball courts have wooden floors.

There are five players on the court for each team. The players must work together to make baskets.

Extra players sit on the bench until it is their turn to play.

Players learn how to **dribble**. To dribble is to **bounce** the ball on the court while standing still or moving. Players cannot move with the ball unless they are dribbling.

Dribbling is an important skill in basketball.

Players also pass the ball
to each other as they try to
move for a shot.

The chest pass and the bounce pass are two types of passes.

Making a basket is harder than it looks. The hoop is 10 feet (3 meters) high!

A basketball hoop has a net underneath the rim.

The team that does not have the ball is on **defense**. They try to keep the other team from making baskets.

Basketball players jump high to make baskets.

The defense has to be careful not to **foul**. The **referee** calls a foul when a player gets bumped or pushed. A player who is fouled might get to shoot **free throws**.

When shooting a free throw, the player cannot step over the free throw line.

Basketball players run a lot. They have to be healthy and fit.

Basketball is a fast game.

Basketball players have to work together as a team in order to win!

It is fun to play basketball on a team.

Glossary

baskets (BASS-kitz): Baskets are when the basketball goes through the hoop. Teams work together to score baskets.

bounce (BOWNSS): To bounce is to push something down so it springs back up again. Basketball players bounce the ball against the ground.

court (KORT): A court is where basketball is played. Ten players are on the court during a basketball game.

defense (DEE-fenss): The defense is the players who are trying to stop the other team from scoring. The defense has to be careful not to foul the other team.

dribble (DRIB-ull): To dribble is to bounce a basketball. Players must dribble the ball as they move down the court.

foul (FOWL): A foul is an action that is against the rules. In basketball, a foul can be called if a player is too rough with another player.

free throws (FREE THROHS): Free throws are shots a player gets to take from behind the free throw line with no one trying to stop him. If a player is fouled, he may get to shoot free throws.

referee (ref-uh-REE): A referee is a person who makes sure the players follow the rules. A referee calls fouls.

To Find Out More

Books

Kalman, Bobbie, and John Crossingham. *Slam Dunk Basketball*. New York: Crabtree, 2007.

Miller, Amanda. *Let's Talk Basketball*. Danbury, CT: Children's Press, 2008.

Stewart, Wayne. *Basketball Facts*. New York: Sterling, 2007.

Thomas, Keltie. *How Basketball Works*. Toronto, Ontario: Maple Tree Press, 2005.

Web Sites

Visit our Web site for links about basketball: *childsworld.com/links*

Note to Parents, Teachers, and Librarians: We routinely verify our Web links to make sure they are safe and active sites. So encourage your readers to check them out!

Index

About the Author

In his long writing career, **Bob Temple** has been a sportswriter and an award-winning author. He has written dozens of books for young readers. Bob owns a development house that specializes in creating children's educational books. He lives with his family in Minnesota.

On the cover: Basketballs and basketball hoops are often bright orange.

Published by The Child's World®
1980 Lookout Drive • Mankato, MN 56003-1705
800-599-READ • www.childsworld.com

ACKNOWLEDGMENTS
The Child's World®: Mary Berendes, Publishing Director
The Design Lab: Design and production
Red Line Editorial: Editorial direction

PHOTO CREDITS: Viorika Prikhodko/iStockphoto, cover; Steve McCabe/iStockphoto, cover; PhotoDisc, 2, 20; Andrew Rich/iStockphoto, 3; ZMUPicture/Shutterstock Images, 5; Shutterstock Images, 7; Rob Friedman/iStockphoto, 9; Pétur Ásgeirsson/Shutterstock Images, 11; Stacy Barnett/Shutterstock Images, 13; Benis Arapovic/Shutterstock Images, 15; Orange Line Media/Shutterstock Images, 17; Rob Belknap/iStockphoto, 19; Rena Schild/Shutterstock Images, 21

Printed in the United States of America in Mankato, Minnesota.
November 2009
F11460

LIBRARY OF CONGRESS CATALOGING-IN-PUBLICATION DATA
Temple, Bob.
 Basketball / by Bob Temple.
  p. cm. — (Jump into sports)
Includes index.
ISBN 978-1-60253-368-4 (library bound : alk. paper)
1. Basketball—Juvenile literature. I. Title. II. Series.
GV885.1.T46 2010
796.323—dc22   2009030585

All sports carry a certain amount of risk. To reduce the risk of injury while playing basketball, play at your own level, wear all safety gear, and use care and common sense. The publisher and author take no responsibility or liability for injuries resulting from playing basketball.